THE WILDERNESS EXPERIENCE

THE WILDERNESS EXPERIENCE

Roszien Kay Lewis

CONFESSIONS PUBLISHING

Scripture quotations marked (NLT) are taken from the *Holy Bible,* New Living Translation © 2004. Wheaton, III: Tyndale House Publisher.

Scripture quotations marked (KJV) are taken from the *Holy Bible*, King James Version.

The Wilderness Experience
Copyright © 2020 Roszien Kay Lewis
ISBN: 978-1-7359620-5-4

Printed and bound in the United States of America.

All Rights Reserved. No part of this publication may be reproduced, stored in a retrieval system, or transmitted, in any form or by any means—electronic, mechanical, photocopying, recording, or otherwise—used in any manner whatsoever without the express written permission of the author, Roszien Kay Lewis.

Editor: Erick Markley

CONFESSIONS PUBLISHING

Confessions Publishing is a subsidiary of Roszien Kay LLC, Lancaster, CA 93536

For information regarding discounts on bulk purchase and all other inquiries, please contact the author directly at roszien@gmail.com or www.roszienkay.com

AUTHOR'S OTHER BOOKS

Confessions of An Overcomer: From Tragedy to Triumph

Confessions of An Overcomer: The Truth About the Wait

Getting Spiritually Snatched

Surrender: Surrendering It All To Gain It All

Submit, Resist, Flee: Strategies To Living A Victorious Life

Hidden Preparation

CONTENTS

INTRODUCTION 9

CHAPTER 1: TO HUMBLE THEE 19

    HOW GOD KNOWS WHETHER OR NOT SOMEONE IS HUMBLE 23

    WE MUST BE HUMBLE BECAUSE JESUS WAS HUMBLE 25

    UNDENIABLE FACTS ABOUT HUMILITY 28

    FALSE HUMILITY 31

    CONSEQUENCES OF BEING PRIDEFUL 35

    HOW DOES GOD HUMBLE US 37

    THE BOTTOM LINE 41

    PRAYER 42

CHAPTER 2: TO PROVE 43

    AM I FAITHFUL? 47

    FALSE FAITH 52

    OVERALL BENEFITS OF PROVING/TESTING 53

    THE BOTTOM LINE 55

    PRAYER 56

CHAPTER 3: WHAT'S IN YOUR HEART? 57

    THE HEART IS NATURALLY EVIL 59

- UNDENIABLE FACTS ABOUT THE HEART 63
- THE BOTTOM LINE: 65
- PRAYER 66

CHAPTER 4: COMMANDMENT KEEPER 67
- WHY IS THERE A STRUGGLE TO OBEY GOD? 70
- IRREFUTABLE FACTS ABOUT OBEDIENCE TO GOD 73
- HOW TO LIVE A LIFE OF OBEDIENCE 77
- THE BOTTOM LINE 78
- PRAYER 79

CONCLUSION 81

ABOUT THE AUTHOR 83

INTRODUCTION

Oftentimes when a believer hears the word "wilderness," one may be overtaken with dread. This is especially true if that particular believer is familiar with being in a wilderness season. Let's be honest for a moment, for one reason or another, no one likes the wilderness! Why is that you ask?!? Let's take a look at the definition of wilderness: "an uncultivated, uninhabited, and inhospitable region."

From reading this, you can see that the wilderness is a place that is unpaved and requires a tremendous amount of work! This is why we dread them.

Let's be honest, we really don't like having to dedicate a lot of time and effort. We don't like experiencing things that will stretch us. Rather, we naturally want to take the easy route as much as possible. Although this is the case, there is always going to be periods in our lives when we have to exert more energy than in others—if we want to get through our wilderness season. This is especially true for the believer. We are constantly on a journey to become more Christ-like.

On this journey, it is inevitable that we will experience wilderness seasons. It doesn't matter how much we try to avoid them either, they will occur.

I know you may be thinking, "what exactly will I experience in a wilderness season?" I'm so relieved and excited that you're thinking this. For a believer, a wilderness season is often seen as experiencing a tough

INTRODUCTION

time. It's a period where one endures discomfort. It's a period where one endures trials and tribulation. The wilderness season is a time of intensified temptations. As well as a time of spiritual attacks. This is why some dread this period.

The wilderness season experienced can present itself in different forms. One person's wilderness experience may involve discomfort and major trials in their finances. For another, it could be a period of some sort of emotional drought where their relationships are heavily affected. While for another, this period may involve matters that are inward and more spiritual in nature. Or someone's wilderness experience can involve all of the above, or something totally different from what's mentioned.

While going through whatever you may be experiencing in your wilderness season, you may be left trying to figure out just how you arrived there. You may question if you have done something wrong. Before you start to drive yourself crazy or panic, calm down. Your wilderness experiences were not necessarily a result of unrepented sin in your life. The wilderness experience is something that every believer will endure throughout life.

It doesn't matter your position in the kingdom of God, either. Your wilderness experience is not determined by age or ethnicity. We all go through them because it's a period of God ordained testing. You read correctly: your past, present, and future wilderness experiences are God-ordained!

In fact, the wilderness experience is often linked to great periods of our lives. One moment things are great. You may be feeling amazing about everything. And then BOOM, things start to spiral in one area or another. This may even

INTRODUCTION

leave you feeling as though you were suddenly tossed into a whirlwind without warning.

As difficult as it may be to come to grips with and believe, it's true. Our wilderness experiences typically follow after a success of some sort. Put another way, the period of testing and trials come on the heels of some period of accomplishment or achievement. Don't believe me? Let's consider the children of Israel. After the Lord had answered their cries and delivered them out of the bondage they had been experiencing in Egypt by miraculously parting the Red Sea and drowning their enemies behind them, it was followed by them journeying in the wilderness.

Yes, their mountain top, or success of being finally freed from bondage after 430 years, was met with a wilderness season. A wilderness season where they were actually tried in an actual wilderness. As a result of them failing the tests of their wilderness season, it ended up lasting for 42 years instead of 2 years.

Because of their rebellion and them struggling against the one that God had put in place to lead them, they were met with more tests, trials, miracles, and provision. This was even done in the face of God cursing some of them. As well as on the heels of God ultimately bringing them out of their wilderness experience.

In my opinion, the children of Israel's wilderness experience was one of the most significant wilderness experiences to date. This is because it was through their experience that we learn why God sends us through this season. According to Deuteronomy 8:2 (KJV), "*And thou shalt remember all the ways which the Lord thy God led thee these forty years in the wilderness, to humble thee, to prove*

INTRODUCTION

thee, to know what was in thine heart, whether thou wouldest keep his commandments, or no."

As awful as the wilderness experience may be or feel, it actually has great purpose. This is why God uses them. He doesn't use them to destroy us. I know that it may be hard for some of you to believe or understand right now, but it's true! I need you to remember that God loves us. He cares for us more than anyone in this world. He cares about our souls.

God is the one that knows us inside out. He knows the exact number of hairs that are on our heads. He knows what we need when we need it. He knows what path we should take in life because He created the path. More importantly, God is the one who knows what has to happen in our lives to get us to exactly where we need to be—the place where He wants us to be.

I know that it may still be hard to believe that wilderness seasons and what you experience there is good for you. I felt the exact same way for years. I couldn't see the benefit of those periods; even though I knew when I crawled out of them (yes, I said crawled) I was better, stronger, and wiser. And not just in the natural, but in the spiritual too.

Honestly, it was only through the revelation of the Holy Spirit that I changed my view of the wilderness. It was only after He ministered to my spirit as I read Deuteronomy 8:2 and the surrounding scripture, that I came to grips with the fact that each wilderness experience I had endured had great purpose. It was in that moment that my thoughts shifted and I accepted the fact that they had all been God-ordained periods meant to: (1) humble me; (2) to prove me; (3) for God to know what was in my heart; (4) and for God to know whether I would keep His commandments.

INTRODUCTION

Once I accepted what had been revealed to me, God directed me to reveal it to His children. Why?!? Our adversary has used the wilderness season as a way to blind believers. He has used it and the experiences that we have had to try to convince us of many untrue things. He has used it to cause us to become emotional and forget the plans and promises of the Lord.

It is my hope that as you read through the proceeding pages, your mind will be transformed by the power of the Holy Spirit. It is my hope that you will no longer dread your wilderness experience. But after reading this book, you will take advantage of them and pass the test of your next wilderness experience!

CHAPTER 1:
TO HUMBLE THEE

Let's be honest, there are things about us that we may not see a problem with. Some of our ways and our personality traits become so embedded in us that we have a difficult time parting with them. Even when they aren't great. What's even worse than our inability to refuse to part with those ways and traits that aren't so great about us, is that those around us accept us the way that we are. They do this by either enabling us, putting up with our antics, or even encouraging us to be who we are, without caring about who doesn't like it!

Unfortunately, there are things about us that people in our lives just put up with. They do this by refusing to say or do things to make us upset. And on the rare occasion that they do build up the courage to voice their concerns about our not-so-great ways or traits, they will abandon their efforts in hopes of "keeping the peace." Or to not push us away from them.

Thankfully, God is not like this. He, unlike those who allow us to continue to walk in error, will not only point out those not-so-great areas in our lives, but He'll orchestrate events in our lives to help us to become better.

I know that you may be wondering, "what does this have to do with anything?" I'm glad that you're wondering this. God will orchestrate things in the wilderness to humble us. He does this because his desire is for us to be humble. You

CHAPTER 1: TO HUMBLE THEE

read correctly! God requires and desires all believers to not only be humble, but He requires us to walk in a spirit of humility on a daily basis. And He requires us to be humble when interacting with everyone that we come into contact with.

According to the King James Version dictionary, to be humble means, "lowly, modest; meek; submissive; opposed to proud, haughty, arrogant or assuming . . . having a low opinion of one's self, and a deep sense of unworthiness in the sight of God." According to the Holman's Bible dictionary it is: "the personal quality of being free from arrogance and pride and having an accurate estimate of one's works."

The humility of believers is of concern to God for several reasons. One of the most important reasons for His concern is that God knows if we are not humble, we will exalt ourselves and become prideful. He knows this because it has already happened before. Yes, you read correctly. One of God's creations, because of the lack of humility, became prideful. This creation that I am referring to is Satan. Satan was one of the most beautiful angels in Heaven. He was powerful as well. As a result of the lack of humility in him, he lacked a sense of unworthiness in the sight of God.

He actually became prideful and wanted to, and thought that he could, be higher than God! As a result of Satan thinking of himself more highly than he was, he had to be cast out of Heaven. He, because of his lack of humility, could no longer be used by God for the purpose for which he was created.

Before you start to turn your nose up at Satan, I need your attention. We have the tendency to do as Satan did. No,

CHAPTER 1: TO HUMBLE THEE

not to try to dethrone God. But we do have the tendency to think that we are worthy of all that God has promised. And in extreme cases, some may even try to exalt themselves higher than Him.

When we aren't humble, God isn't able to do all that He wants to do for us and through us. When we aren't humble, we run the risk of trying to steal God's glory. And act as if we do not need Him.

But God, in His infinite wisdom and design, uses the wilderness to help us to not fall into pride as Satan did. He uses it to humble us!

HOW GOD KNOWS WHETHER OR NOT SOMEONE IS HUMBLE

The spirit of humility is typically offered in a spirit of respect, submission, and obedience. Humility is not merely an outward demeanor, it's a heart attitude. That's why it's safe to say that humility is inward. Humility is genuine. It's not a performance that is witnessed by others, either. However, when you are truly humble inwardly, it will show on the outside.

God knows whether or not someone is humble by the condition of one's heart. It's not based on our outer appearance because the appearance of it can be faked. Although we can trick others by doing good deeds as if it's done with a heart of humility, we cannot trick or fool God because He looks at what's inside of our hearts.

"A good person produces good things from the treasury of a good heart, and an evil person produces evil things from the treasury of an evil heart…"
(LUKE 6:45 NLT)

CHAPTER 1: TO HUMBLE THEE

WE MUST BE HUMBLE BECAUSE JESUS WAS HUMBLE

God requires all believers to be Christ-like. Jesus, although He was God in the flesh and the living Word, was humble. No matter what happened while He was here on earth, He never thought of Himself as being higher than others. He never treated anyone wrong because He was the Son of God. Rather, He served with a spirit of meekness. He even washed the feet of the disciples while He was with them.

Rejoice greatly, O daughter of Zion! Shout aloud, O daughter of Jerusalem! Behold, your king is coming to you; righteous and having salvation is he, humble and mounted on a donkey, on a colt, the foal of a donkey."
(Zechariah 9:9 NLT)

5 You must have the same attitude that Christ Jesus had 6Though he was God, he did not think of equality with God as something to cling to. 7Instead, he gave up his divine privileges; he took the humble position of a slave and was born as a human being. When he appeared in human form, 8 he humbled himself in obedience to God and died a criminal's death on a cross. 9 Therefore, God elevated him to the place of highest honor and gave him the name above all other names, 10 that at the name of Jesus every knee should bow, in heaven and on earth and under the earth, 11 and every tongue declare that Jesus Christ is Lord, to the glory of God the Father.

(Philippians 2:5-11 NLT)

"For even the Son of Man came not to be served but to serve others and to give his life as a ransom for many."

(Mark 10:45 NLT)

Those who say they live in God should live their lives as Jesus did.

(1 John 2:6 NLT)

"For God called you to do good, even if it means suffering, just as Christ suffered for you. He is your example, and you must follow in his steps."

(1 Peter 2:21 NLT)

CHAPTER 1: TO HUMBLE THEE

"Therefore be imitators of God, as beloved children. And walk in love, as Christ loved us and gave himself up for us, a fragrant offering a sacrifice to God."

(Ephesians 5:1-2 NLT)

"You call me Teacher and Lord, and you are right, for so I am. If I then, your Lord and Teacher, have washed your feet, you also ought to wash one another's feet. For I have given you an example, that you also should do just as I have done to you. Truly, truly, I say to you, a servant is not greater than his master, nor is a messenger greater than the one who sent him. If you know these things, blessed are you if you do them."

(John 13:13-17 NLT)

UNDENIABLE FACTS ABOUT HUMILITY

1. Humility is necessary for repentance.

The sacrifice you desire is a broken spirit. You will not reject a broken and repentant heart, O God.

(Psalm 51:17 NLT)

2. Because God chose you, you must be humble.

"Since God chose you to be the holy people he loves, you must clothe yourselves with tenderhearted mercy, kindness, humility, gentleness, and patience.

(Colossians 3:12 NLT)

3. God will honor you if you're humble.

"So humble yourselves under the mighty power of God, and at the right time he will lift you up in honor.

(1Peter 5:6 NLT)

4. God gives grace to the humble.

And he gives grace generously. As the Scriptures say, "God opposes the proud but gives grace to the humble."'

(James 4:6 NLT)

CHAPTER 1: TO HUMBLE THEE

5. Humility will turn the wrath of God.

"Because Rehoboam humbled himself, the LORD's anger was turned away, and he did not destroy him completely. There were still some good things in the land of Judah."

(2 Chronicles 12:12 NLT)

6. God will help you when you are humble.

"If people are in trouble and you say, 'Help them,' God will save them."

(Job 22:29 NLT)

"Then if my people who are called by my name will humble themselves and pray and seek my face and turn from their wicked ways, I will hear from heaven and will forgive their sins and restore their land."

(2 Chronicles 7:14 NLT)

7. God humiliates those who refuse to be humble.

"You rescue the humble, but you humiliate the proud."
(Psalm 18:27 NLT)

8. God takes pleasure in those who display humility.

"For the LORD delights in his people; he crowns the humble with victory."
(Psalm 149:4 NLT)

9. Humility will cause you to see others as more significant.

"Don't be selfish; don't try to impress others. Be humble, thinking of others as better than yourselves. 4 Don't look out only for your own interests, but take an interest in others, too.
(Philippians 2:3-4 NLT)

CHAPTER 1: TO HUMBLE THEE

10. Wisdom comes with humility.

"Pride leads to disgrace, but with humility comes wisdom."
(Proverbs 11:2 NLT)

11. Humility will result in us walking down the right path.

"He leads the humble in doing right, teaching them his way."
(Psalm 25:9)

FALSE HUMILITY

The Lord frowns upon those who display false humility. False humility is pridefulness in disguise. Pride is, "a high or inordinate opinion of one's own dignity, importance, merit or superiority, whether as cherished in the mind or as displayed in bearing, conduct, etc" (dictionary.com). It's okay to take pride in something or someone. However, pride becomes an issue when it becomes a lofty and arrogant assumption of superiority.

If you'd recall earlier I mentioned that God looks on the heart of a person to determine whether or not they are humble. This is how God is able to determine whether someone has crossed the line when it comes to being proud of oneself and becoming lofty, arrogant, or feeling superior to others. And this is how He determines whether or not someone is truly humble or displaying false humility.

There are people who intentionally devalue themselves and their contributions in an attempt to appear humble. What do I mean by this?!? There are people who will falsely portray themselves as helpless or having a lack of power. Individuals who display false humility also have the tendency of deflecting praise in hopes of getting it. Some even will fish for compliments to draw attention to

CHAPTER 1: TO HUMBLE THEE

themselves. And some even talk about how humble they are to prove that they are humble. I'm not saying that everyone who says that they are humble are displaying false humility, what I am saying is that those that display false humility will say it as well.

It's often difficult for men to know whether or not someone is truly humble. This is because we are only able to see what someone portrays. We are only able to judge—without revelation by the Holy Spirit—based on the outer appearance of a person. Thankfully, if a person that displays false humility is watched long enough, their fruits (their actions) will start to speak for them. They will produce that which is in their hearts after a while. Why?!? Because they won't be able to continue to keep up the act.

Those who display false humanity are actually prideful. Someone who is prideful has an excessively high opinion of oneself. It stems from self-righteousness or conceit. Pride leads to a person giving themselves the credit for something that God accomplished through them. Pride leads to one taking God's glory and keeping it for themselves.

Pride is a hindrance in our efforts to seek God with our entire hearts. This is why pride is sinful and hated by God. Pride keeps people from accepting Jesus as their Lord and Savior because pride causes people to not recognize that they cannot do anything without Jesus. And it leads to an inability to see that without Him, we are nothing.

CHAPTER 1: TO HUMBLE THEE

CONSEQUENCES OF BEING PRIDEFUL

1. Pridefulness is a sin.

"Haughty eyes, a proud heart, and evil actions are all sin."
(Proverbs 21:4 NLT)

2. Pridefulness will lead to destruction.

"Pride goes before destruction, and haughtiness before a fall."
(Proverbs 16:18 NLT)

3. Pridefulness leads to punishment.

"The Lord detests the proud; they will surely be punished"
(Proverbs 16:5 NLT)

4. Pridefulness is not of God.

"For the world offers only a craving for physical pleasure, a craving for everything we see, and pride in our

achievements and possessions, These are not from the Father, but are from this world."

(1 John 2:16 NLT)

5. Pridefulness is a result of deception.

"If you think you are too important to help someone, you are only fooling yourself. You are not that important."

(Galatians 6:3 NLT)

6. Pridefulness leaves you hopeless.

"There is more hope for fools than for people who think they are wise."

(Proverbs 26:12 NLT)

7. Pridefulness results in no good.

"It's not good to eat much honey, and it's not good to seek honor for yourself."

(Proverbs 25:26 NLT)

CHAPTER 1: TO HUMBLE THEE

HOW DOES GOD HUMBLE US

As we continue down this journey called life, we are always being processed by the Lord. Mainly because He wants to make sure that our hearts stay as pure as possible before Him. He wants to make sure that we don't become prideful or think that we no longer need Him.

God has several ways of humbling us. Below is a list of some of those ways.

God Develops Humility In Us Through Suffering

One way in which God humbles us is through our wilderness experience. He will allow us to experience suffering of some sort. To get a better understanding of what I mean by this, let's take a look at the definition of suffer : *"to submit to or be forced to endure; to undergo, experience; to endure death, pain, or distress; to sustain loss or damage..."*

I know that suffering is a topic that many believers shy away from. Mainly because no one really wants to suffer. And some have been led to believe that once you receive Jesus Christ as your Lord and Savior, everything will be great all the time. Unfortunately, this is one of the biggest misconceptions of living for Christ!

The reality is this: living for Christ means that you will suffer! Don't believe me? Consider the following passages of Scripture:

CHAPTER 1: TO HUMBLE THEE

"21 For God called you to do good, even if it means suffering, just as Christ suffered for you. He is your example, and you must follow in his steps. 22 He never sinned nor deceived anyone.

23 He did not retaliate when he was insulted, nor threaten revenge when he suffered.

He left his case in the hands of God, who always judges fairly."
(1 Peter 2:21-23 NLT)

Although you may experience some type of suffering during the journey of humility, it is well worth it! Everything that we endure as believers will always work for our good if we allow God to justify us and bring us forth.

In fact, if we suffer with Christ, we will reign with Him. This is why we must go through it, no matter how much we hate it. Remember, the goal is to test us to see whether or not we will be humble enough to rely on Him.

"If we suffer, we shall also reign with him…"
(2 Timothy 2:12 KJV)

God Develops Humility In Us Through the Gospel

As we read through the gospel, we are constantly confronted with the fact that without our Lord and Savior, we are sinful and deserving of death. As we flip through the pages of the Bible, we cannot help but to be faced with the reality that our sins are great; because of this, we are unworthy of the blessings that God bestows upon us. As well as the fact that we are unworthy of the blessing of salvation which was obtained by Jesus Christ—the only perfect one that walked this earth.

God Develops Humanity in Us Through Us Reaping What We've Sown

Our actions produce many consequences. Some good and some bad. But when God gives us something that we do not deserve, it causes us to realize how amazing He is. It also

CHAPTER 1: TO HUMBLE THEE

forces us to admit how unworthy we are. His kindness causes us to become meek and humble.

On the flip side, when God allows us to reap the things that we deserve, it humbles us as well. The truth is this: some consequences will cause us to admit that we are nothing—that we need Jesus more than we expected.

THE BOTTOM LINE

God knows that our lack of humility limits the release of blessings in our life. It also stifles our advancement. God is not okay with this because He has promised us many blessings in His Word that He wants to reveal to us.

Therefore, God uses the wilderness experience to humble us. He knows that humility is something that's gained through experience. God knows that without Him thrusting us into seasons of humbling, we would not do it on our own. So, He allows us to go through these seasons in the wilderness because He sees the benefit of them.

Although we may not like it, it's for our good. Humbling seasons in our lives will produce greater good fruit within us. It will also help us to see how much we really need the Lord.

PRAYER

Lord, help me to remain humble! And as you allow me to go through seasons where you're humbling me, give me the grace to not fight against what you're doing within me. Give me eyes to see the error of my ways if there are any. Father, help me to go through the process without dread. Give me the strength to hold on to you and to go through it until you're done processing me. In Jesus' mighty name. Amen!

CHAPTER 2:
TO PROVE

God allows some wilderness seasons in our lives to prove us. To prove means, *"to establish the truth or genuineness of . . ."* The definition of the Hebrew word nasah, means to prove, to test and to try. This term refers to God testing the faithfulness of human beings. But not just any faithfulness, faithfulness to God.

You may be wondering why God would use the wilderness season as a time to test whether or not we will remain faithful—especially when we have proclaimed and shown Him that we are faithful. Well, the truth is that our faithfulness to God cannot only be measured by what we do when things are going well. The reason being is that it's easy to be faithful and dedicated to someone or something when everything is going smoothly. It's easy to serve God when we are in a season when we are experiencing His blessings and protection, when everything is going according to our plans and desires.

God allows some wilderness seasons in our lives to give us a chance to show Him whether or not we are really faithful to Him. He allows it to test whether or not we will still proclaim that HE is good when all hell is breaking out around us. He also allows it to show us where we are as well.

The truth of the matter is this: a person that will be faithful to God no matter the circumstance is hard to find. Don't believe it? Consider Proverbs 20:6, *"Most men will proclaim each his own goodness but who can find a faithful man?"*

CHAPTER 2: TO PROVE

Before we go any further, we must arrive at a clear understanding of what faithfulness means. According to several definitions, faithfulness means, *"fidelity; loyalty, firm adherence to allegiance and duty..."* God is literally trying to prove whether or not you are committed to adhering to Him.

So, He uses the wilderness period to prove whether or not you're going to live to please Him or people. He even uses it to see whether you will run back to idols once things aren't going your way. Will you rely on that person that He told you to break ties with? Will you run to alcohol, back to fornicating, smoking weed, or watching pornography when you're stressed, and things aren't going your way? Or will you press into prayer and read His word more? Will you place something else as being of a higher priority than Him because things aren't going your way? Will you stop professing and loving according to the gospel, just because you're being persecuted? Or will you continue to stay focused and forsake everything to continue to pursue Him?

Faithfulness is based upon what we value, combined with what we are committed to. Let's be honest, we have the tendency to be faithful to what we deem important. God knows this. So, He allows us to experience the wilderness period from time to time to see whether or not He is important to us!

God does this because faithfulness is very valuable to Him. Why?!? Because He is faithful. He's faithful to His promises. He's faithful to His own laws. And He's faithful to mankind, even though we aren't always faithful.

Although there are times that believers aren't faithful, it's still important. Why?!? Because we are to be imitators to

CHAPTER 2: TO PROVE

God. This means that we must strive to be faithful to God above all else. Not just sometimes either, but all the time, and in every situation.

The truth of the matter is this: God will not tolerate unfaithfulness. He will not be in competition with anything or anyone else. Remember, He is a jealous God (Exodus 34:14). Therefore, He requires us to forsake everyone and everything else and come after Him!

> *"If you want to be my disciple, you must, by comparison, hate everyone else—your father and mother, wife and children, brothers and sisters—yes even your own life. Otherwise, you cannot be my disciple."*
> *(Luke 14:26 NLT)*

AM I FAITHFUL?

Below is a list of questions to consider when evaluating whether or not you are faithful to God.

1. Will you abandon Him?

Before you answer this question, think about what the disciples did after Jesus' trial and crucifixion. They followed Peter and went fishing after Jesus' death and resurrection. I'm pretty sure that they would have never imagined that they would do this. But they did.

I highlight this to show you how challenging this could be. However, no matter how challenging it may be to not abandon Jesus during the times of the unknown, as you are in your wilderness season, you must push past the urge to. You must remain faithful even when you cannot trace Him. You must remain faithful when things around you aren't lining up with what He said!

CHAPTER 2: TO PROVE

2. Do you love Him more than you love what you have?

You must be willing to let go of everything that you possess if Jesus asks you to. You cannot be so tied to things that you refuse to obey God. Faithfulness requires your willingness to release whatever you have in your possession at the drop of a dime.

3. Do you love Him above all?

As stated previously, God is a jealous God. He doesn't want you to love anything or anyone more than, or as much as, you love Him. Not even our children, family members, spouses, or friends. Why?!? Because when we love others more than Him, our love for them has the potential to interfere with our relationship with Him.

4. Will you forsake others for Him?

Part of following Christ is leaving everyone and everything behind if asked. Although you may not be asked to do it, you must always be willing to. You must be willing to obey God and end relationships if He instructs you to. You must also be willing to leave family or friends behind as Abraham did.

5. Will you follow Him down the narrow road?

Being faithful to God means that you will travel a path that many don't want to take—a path that requires you to be Christ-like. On this road, you're required to die to self daily. You're required to forsake the world. This narrow road is often lonely. Traveling down it will cause you to be misunderstood.

CHAPTER 2: TO PROVE

6. Will you obey the leading of the Holy Spirit?

The Holy Spirit is Who God gave us to lead, guide, teach, and comfort us. He is the Spirit of God that dwells within us. Because of this, He is the one that knows the mind of God. And He knows what we should do.

Let's face it, without the leading of the Holy Spirit, we are incapable of truly being faithful to God on our own. Therefore, if we are to be faithful and remain faithful to God, we must allow Him to lead us. And we must do so on a regular basis if we are to grow in our faithfulness to God.

FALSE FAITH

There are times when we may appear to have faith in God. However, when trials and tests hit our lives, we fall apart and crumble. We may even run in the opposite direction. This often occurs because of false faith. And it happens because we cannot stand to be tested.

If you can relate to this, don't feel bad. We have all been there a time or two. In all honesty, this is why we need to go through the wilderness experience to build us up, so that we may become faithful to God no matter the hardship, marital problems, and whatever else is thrown at us.

What you must understand is that the testing that you will endure during this wilderness experience:

CHAPTER 2: TO PROVE

1. Is a part of God's plan.

2. Puts God's power on display in your life (it actually results in Him proving Himself and His Word).

3. Prepares you for service.

4. Helps to sanctify you; and

5. Helps you to lean, depend, and rely on God more.

OVERALL BENEFITS OF PROVING/TESTING

Just as there are benefits to passing tests in the natural realm, there are benefits to passing tests in the spirit realm. Below are some of those benefits:

1. God Rewards Us

When we pass the test, God rewards us because He knows that our faith is in Him alone.

"These trials will show that your faith is genuine. It is being tested as fire tests and purifies gold—though your faith is far more precious than mere gold. So when your faith remains strong through many trials, it will bring you much praise and glory and honor on the day when Jesus Christ is revealed to the whole world."

(1 Peter 1:7 NLT)

"God blesses those who patiently endure testing and temptation. Afterwards they will receive the crown of life that God has promised to those who love him."

(James 1:12 NLT)

2. We Grow

When we are tested, we grow in endurance, character, strength, and patience.

CHAPTER 2: TO PROVE

"We rejoice, too, when we run into problems and trials, for we know that they help us develop endurance. 4 And endurance develops strength of character, and character strengthens our confident hope of salvation. 5 And this hope will not lead to disappointment. For we know how dearly God loves us, because he has given us the Holy Spirit to fill our hearts with his love."

(Romans 5:3-5 NLT)

"In his kindness God called you to share in his eternal glory by means of Christ Jesus. So after you have suffered a little while, he will restore, support, and strengthen you, and he will place you on a firm foundation."

(1 Peter 5:10 NLT)

THE BOTTOM LINE

As God allows us to go into a season in the wilderness to prove us, as long as we remain faithful we will come out better. As we stand committed to Him, despite the adversity that may be experienced, He will strengthen us along the journey.

We must keep our eyes on Him no matter what. We must be willing to obey Him at every turn. And we must understand that God has entrusted us with the experience because He knows that we are equipped to survive the wilderness season of proving our faithfulness to Him.

PRAYER

Lord, as you take me through the process of refining me, help me to stay faithful. Help me to remain rooted and grounded in you as I forsake everything else. Father, for the moments that I may waiver in my faithfulness to you, continue to show me mercy and grace. Father, strengthen me in every area that I may be weak in as I continue to press forward during my wilderness season. In Jesus' mighty name. Amen!

CHAPTER 3:
WHAT'S IN YOUR HEART?

Knowing the posture of our heart is extremely important to God. Mainly because our heart determines whether or not we will obey Him! This is why the Lord allows us to go into the wilderness season—to examine our hearts.

The heart is the spiritual part of us. It's the part where our emotions and desires dwell. In its natural state and condition, the human heart is evil. It's treacherous. And it's deceitful. According to Jeremiah 17:9 (NLT), *"The human heart is the most deceitful of all things, and desperately wicked. Who really knows how bad it is?"*

God is the only one who knows the condition of our heart. He understands it, and He knows the secrets that lie within it. Because He knows what's in our hearts, He judges it righteously.

"God would surely have known it, for he knows the secrets of every heart."

(Psalm 44:21 NLT)

"But I, the Lord, search all hearts and examine secret motives. I give all people their due rewards, according to what their actions deserve."

(Jeremiah 17:10 NLT)

"People may be right in their own eyes, but the Lord examines their hearts."

(Proverbs 21:2 NLT)

CHAPTER 3: WHAT'S IN YOUR HEART?

"But the Lord said to Samuel, "Don't judge by his appearance or height, for I have rejected him. The Lord doesn't see things the way you see them. People judge by outward appearance, but the Lord looks at the heart."

(1 Samuel 16:7 NLT)

THE HEART IS NATURALLY EVIL

The heart, when in an unregenerated state, is evil. This is due to our sin nature. Although this is the case, it was not always like this. When God created Adam and Eve, He created them in His image and likeness with a pure heart. This means that they were perfect. Their nature was not sinful.

However, when they decided to disobey God and eat from the tree of the knowledge of good and evil, sin entered into them. When this happened, their entire nature was changed from being perfect to now being corrupted with sin—including their heart.

Sadly, their decision to disobey God did not only affect them. It affected mankind. Instead of being born in the image of God, mankind is born in the image of Adam. Before you close the book or even try to refute what I am saying, considering Genesis 5:3 (KJV), which says: *"And Adam lived an hundred and thirty years, and begat a son in his own likeness, after his image; and called his name Seth."* Sin was literally imputed to all of us.

Still not convinced? Consider the Scriptures below:

"When Adam sinned, sin entered the world. Adam's sin brought death, so death spread to everyone, for everyone sinned."

(Romans 5:12 NLT)

***"Yes, Adam's one sin brings condemnation for everyone**, but Christ's one act of righteousness brings a right relationship with God and new life for everyone."*

(Romans 5:18 NLT)

CHAPTER 3: WHAT'S IN YOUR HEART?

"Just as everyone dies because we all belong to Adam, everyone who belongs to Christ will be given new life"

(1 Corinthians 15:22)

Although this was the case, God had a plan to redeem mankind back to Him. He sent Jesus Christ to die for our sins, so that through Him, we could be reconciled back to Him. And now when we are conformed to the image of Christ, we are restored back to the image of God. This results in regeneration—*"new birth by the grace of God; that change by which the will and natural enmity of man to God and his law are subdued, and a principle of supreme love to God and his law, or holy affections, are implanted in the heart (KJV dictionary).*

In order for regeneration to occur, we must accept Jesus Christ as our Lord and Savior. In order words, we must accept the free gift of salvation that is offered to us by Him. When we do this, our hearts are now changed. Meaning, where it was unwilling to obey God, it is now willing to obey Him, surrender to Him, and submit to Him.

Although our heart is changed when we get saved, there is still a process of purification that we must go through throughout our lives. Why?!? Because there is always a battle being waged within us. Our Spirit is in constant war with our flesh. At times, war produces heart issues.

Despite the fact that we will sometimes struggle with heart issues, God is faithful because He helps us. God constantly works towards creating a new heart in us by testing our hearts. He doesn't just require that we figure things out on our own. And He allows the Holy Spirit to convict our hearts.

CHAPTER 3: WHAT'S IN YOUR HEART?

UNDENIABLE FACTS ABOUT THE HEART

1. We must guard our hearts.

"Guard your heart above all else, for it determines the course of your life."

(Proverbs 4:23 NLT)

2. Our heart is made new through testing.

"You have tested my thoughts and examined my heart in the night. You have scrutinized me and found nothing wrong. I am determined not to sin in what I say."

(Psalm 17:3 NLT)

3. A new heart is only given to us by God.

"And I will give you a new heart, and I will put a new spirit in you. I will take out your stony, stubborn heart and give you a tender, responsive heart."

(Ezekiel 36:26 NLT)

"Create in me a clean heart, O God. Renew a loyal spirit within me."

(Psalm 51:10 NLT)

4. When our heart seeks God, we find Him.

"If you look for me wholeheartedly you will find me."

(Jeremiah 29:13 NLT)

5. Our heart is where we hide God's Word.

"I have hidden your word in my heart, that might not sin against you."

(Psalm 119:11 NLT)

6. Our hearts produce fruit in our lives.

"A good person produces good things from the treasury of a good heart, and an evil person produces evil things from the treasury of an evil heart. What you say flows from what is in your heart."

(Luke 6:45 NLT)

CHAPTER 3: WHAT'S IN YOUR HEART?

"For from within, out of a person's heart, come evil thoughts, sexual immorality, theft, murder, 22 adultery, greed, wickedness, deceit, lustful desires, envy, slander, pride and foolishness. 23 All these vile things come from within; they are what defile you."

(Mark 7:21-23 NLT)

THE BOTTOM LINE:

The Lord uses our wilderness season to test what's in our hearts. Yes, God definitely already knows what is in our hearts because He is omniscient—He's all knowing. Therefore, He allows the testing to bring to light through evidence what is truly in our hearts. In order words, He'll allow the testing of the heart to be done in the wilderness to manifest that which is in the inside of us.

Although it may not feel good, it's for our good. Don't throw in the towel! Let go of anything that God is trying to work out of your heart. And more importantly, remember God is with you!

PRAYER

Father, search my heart. Whatever is not like you, whatever is not pleasing to you, whatever is keeping me from fully surrendering to you, remove it. Father, any stony area—the area that is disobedient to Your voice—that you may find as you test my heart, please remove it. If you discover any prideful areas during your inspection, Father, remove it.

Abba, I want to be pleasing to you. I don't want to miss that which you intend to write on the table of my heart during my wilderness season. So, I lift my heart to you, for you to mold and shape it. And I thank you, Lord, for all that You're doing in me during this season. In Jesus' name, Amen.

CHAPTER 4: COMMANDMENT KEEPER

Whether or not we'll keep God's commandments is of great importance. Not only does it determine what God is able to do in us and through us while we are here on earth, but it determines where we will spend eternity. As a result, God has created the wilderness experience to test whether or not we'll keep his commandments.

Before we can move further, we must take a look at what is a commandment. According to the King James Version Dictionary, a commandment is: *a command; a mandate; an order or injunction given by authority; charge; precept."*

When we consider the commandments that God is trying to see whether or not we will keep, it's beyond the Ten commandments written in the Bible. Rather, God is testing to see whether or not we will obey everything that He tells us to do. He wants to know whether we will execute his charge. He wants to know whether we will accept the mandate that He has given to us and placed upon our lives.

The best way for God to see if someone will obey is by testing them. In fact, testing to see whether or not the children of Israel would obey His commandment was of great importance to God. In Deuteronomy 5:27 (NLT), they told Moses, *"Go yourself and listen to what the LORD our God says. Then come and tell us everything he tells you and we will listen."* From this verse you see that the children of Israel made a vow to obey whatever God would tell Moses.

CHAPTER 4: COMMANDMENT KEEPER

If you'd be honest, you would have to admit that you too have done the same thing. Truthfully, all believers have made a vow to obey. And we've done this without knowing what God would say.

At the time of our decision, we were committed to following through with our confession. Mainly because our spirits, which are committed to God from the moment we receive salvation, was willing. Unfortunately, one thing that we often ignore when making this confession is that there is still a part of us that is not so willing to obey whatever God will say—our flesh.

Although we did not consider this, God did. He knows that our flesh is unwilling to submit to Him. God knows that our flesh is hostile to Him and His commandments. This is why He uses the wilderness to test whether or not we will truly keep His commandments.

The wilderness really allows God to see if we are just offering Him lip service, or whether we will put in the necessary work to obey His commandments. It's only when the heat is turned up in our lives through trials and tribulation that we can really know for sure whether or not we will obey God or obey our flesh. The truth is this, it's easy to obey God when things are going well in our lives. However, it's not so easy to obey Him when things are in disarray, when we want to reject His commandments, and when our back is up against the wall.

WHY IS THERE A STRUGGLE TO OBEY GOD?

As mentioned previously, we struggle with obeying God, although our spirit is willing, because of our flesh. Our flesh is weak. It doesn't not want to do what is right. It prefers to do what feels good—those things that bring it

CHAPTER 4: COMMANDMENT KEEPER

great pleasure. So, it causes us to wrestle with whether we will obey God, even though we truly want to in our hearts.

Even though there are times that we are caught up in this struggle, we must still decide to obey God. Yes, it's hard. Yes, it will take much effort. No, the struggle between our flesh will never go away. But the more we decide to say no to our flesh in order to obey God's commandments, the easier it will be for us to keep and obey God's commandments the next time!

Another reason we struggle with whether or not we will keep and obey God's commandments is because we don't like to sacrifice. There are times when obeying what God has commanded of us will mean that we will have to sacrifice some things. Yes, God will require us to give up some things that we will want to keep, in order for us to do what He wants us to do.

If you'd be honest, the struggle to keep and obey God's commandments is real! Although this is a proven fact, we must strive to obey Him. Honestly, the struggles we experience are actually for our benefit. They help to work those things out of us that aren't useful. They create an awareness of what we need to work on. They reveal to us our areas of growth. And they result in us being Christ-like.

> *"And I know that nothing good lives in me, that is, in my sinful nature. I want to do what is right, but I can't."*
> *(Romans 7:18 NLT)*

> *"For the sinful nature is always hostile to God. It never did obey God's law. And it never will."*
> *(Romans 8:7 NLT)*

> *"The sinful nature wants to do evil, which is just the opposite of what the Spirit wants. And the Spirit gives us desires that are the opposite of what the sinful nature desires. These two forces are constantly fighting each other, so you are not free to carry out your good intentions."*
> *(Galatians 5:17 NLT)*

CHAPTER 4: COMMANDMENT KEEPER

"Dear friends, I warn you as "temporary residents and foreigners" to keep away from worldly desires that wage war against your very souls."

(1 Peter 2:11 NLT)

"But Samuel replied, "What is more pleasing to the LORD: your burnt offerings and sacrifices or your obedience to his voice? Listen! Obedience is better than sacrifice, and submission is better than offering the fat of rams."

(1Samuel 15:22 NLT)

IRREFUTABLE FACTS ABOUT OBEDIENCE TO GOD

God desires for believers to obey Him and Him only. Yes, he did give us the choice to choose whether or not we will obey Him. But He wants us to use that freewill to choose to obey Him and His commandments for the following reasons:

1. **Obedience to God leads to a life of eternity with Him.**

   Obedience to God causes us to turn away from sin and pleasing our flesh and fulfilling its lusts. It results in us fulfilling the Lord's will and desires. Which in turn results in us being able to experience Him.

2. **Obedience to God shows where your trust lies.**

   Obeying God is not always easy. Sometimes what He tells us to do is scary. Some of His instructions will not make sense at all. And sometimes we won't be able to see where it will lead. So, when we obey Him, we show Him that we are placing our confidence in Him and Him alone. Our obedience shows that we place our trust in Him and not in our feelings, our sight, or our own desires. This pleases God.

3. Your obedience to God allows God to see if He can trust you with more.

When we obey God, it shows Him that He can trust us. Every time that we obey Him, it proves to Him that we aren't just offering lip service. In turn, God is able to trust us with more assignments, more tests, and trials, as well as His secrets.

4. Obedience to God will result in you fulfilling your God given purpose.

God is the one who created us. He has a great plan for each of us. We all were created to fulfill His purpose in this earth. Obeying Him will result in us fulfilling it!

When we decide to obey God, we are led on the right path in life because we've allowed His voice to be our guide. As a result, no matter how much we may have to struggle, no matter how many closed doors we may encounter, we will ALWAYS arrive on the doorstep of purpose!

5. Obedience to God results in Him releasing blessings in your life.

When we obey God, He releases unimaginable blessings in our lives. This occurs even though we don't obey God to get stuff, we obey Him to be pleasing to Him!

When God sees that we will obey Him, He gives to us out of His abundance as He sees fit. For one it may be healing their body. For another it may be finances. For others it may be an inheritance, strategies for one's business, vision where there was spiritual blindness, assignments, territories, peace, joy, as well as other things.

HOW TO LIVE A LIFE OF OBEDIENCE

In order to live a life of obedience that transcends our own ability, we must be filled with God's Spirit. In Ezekiel 36:27 (NLT), God said, *"And I will put my Spirit in you so that you will follow my decrees and be careful to obey my regulations."* Just as God promised to do this for Ezekiel, He'll do it for any believer who asks for His Spirit—the Holy Spirit— to come and dwell within them.

Truthfully, we all need to ask for and receive the Holy Spirit. Without Him, we will not be able to fulfill the commandments of the Lord. Without the indwelling of the Holy Spirit, we will hit and miss when going through the wilderness. He is the only one that gives us the power to obey. And He is the one that knows all things—that means He remembers what the Lord has commanded of us even when we don't.

But you have to make obeying the Holy Spirit a priority in your life. You must do so even when you don't want to.

THE BOTTOM LINE

Although God places us in the wilderness to see whether or not we will obey His commandments, we must be sure that we do so. Our obedience to God is of great importance. It separates us from those who don't live for Him or believe in Him. It shows Him that we really love and trust Him. And it leads to Him bestowing upon us many great things.

The next time you're faced with whether or not to obey God when you're going through a difficult season, muster

CHAPTER 4: COMMANDMENT KEEPER

up all the strength that you have and OBEY Him. It will be well worth it in the end!

PRAYER

Father, help me to fulfill every commandment that you give to me. When I don't want to obey you, God give me the strength to obey you. Lord, remove the desire within me to hold on to that which I am able to see, so that I can see what you're trying to show me. Father, help me to trust you even when I cannot trace you! In the name of Jesus. Amen.

CONCLUSION

The wilderness season is the number one season that believers dislike. It's a season that God uses to really test and try us. It's the season where we may experience some of our greatest pain.

Despite the fact that we dislike wilderness seasons so much, it's one of the most important seasons in the life of a believer. It's the season where God humbles us. It's the season where He proves us. It's the season where He shows us what's really in our hearts. And puts us in situations to see whether or not we will obey His commandments.

Although the wilderness season isn't pleasant by any means, we must go through it and get through it. Why?!? Because it's a season that has the potential of resulting in us evolving . . .

No matter how hard you want to give up while you're in your wilderness, you can't. There's too much for you to learn during this period. And there's so much that God wants to reveal to you.

Therefore, it's important for you to hold on to God, His commands, and your faith as God takes you through your wilderness season!

ABOUT THE AUTHOR

Roszien Kay Lewis — Juris Doctor, speaker and entrepreneur— is an emerging leader and catalyst with a prophetic voice. She has a deep rooted desire to see people healed, delivered, and set free. As a result she founded Destined to Be Released Ministries, a ministry whose sole objective is to encourage, teach, and equip others through the Word of God. Roszien has hosted conferences, workshops, and spearheads the "21 Day Jump Start My Draw" prayer challenge.

As a result of the trauma she suffered in her childhood and teenage years, Roszien formed #ConfessionsOfAnOvercomer motivational speaking company. Through this company she shares her testimony of overcoming every obstacle in her life.

And she encourages others that they too can overcome anything as long as they believe in themselves.

When Roszien is not ministering to or mentoring others, she's busy assisting others with book publishing. She is the sole owner of Confessions Publishing, a Christian based publishing company that assists authors with "turning their manuscripts into a masterpiece."

Roszien resides in California with her two beautiful daughters.

CONTACT ROSZIEN

FACEBOOK: ROSZIEN KAY LEWIS

IG: ROSZIEN KAY LEWIS

EMAIL: roszien@gmail.com

Website : Roszienkay.com

www.ingramcontent.com/pod-product-compliance
Lightning Source LLC
Chambersburg PA
CBHW051711040426
42446CB00008B/820